Feathers on my Wings.

BUILDING BLOCKS FOR HIGH FLYING GLOBAL CAREER

FOR YOUNG EXECUTIVES AND EMERGING BUSINESS LEADERS

Vivek Puranik

Copyright © Vivek Puranik 2023
All Rights Reserved.

ISBN 979-8-89026-744-3

This book has been published with all efforts taken to make the material error-free after the consent of the author. However, the author and the publisher do not assume and hereby disclaim any liability to any party for any loss, damage, or disruption caused by errors or omissions, whether such errors or omissions result from negligence, accident, or any other cause.

While every effort has been made to avoid any mistake or omission, this publication is being sold on the condition and understanding that neither the author nor the publishers or printers would be liable in any manner to any person by reason of any mistake or omission in this publication or for any action taken or omitted to be taken or advice rendered or accepted on the basis of this work. For any defect in printing or binding the publishers will be liable only to replace the defective copy by another copy of this work then available.

DEDICATION

This book is dedicated to –

- **Suhasini Puranik,** my mother, and my management guru.
- **Parameshwar Puranik,** my father, and my ethical compass.
- **P. Venkat Narayan,** for being my first boss.
- **Suraj Thodimarath,** for demonstrating what it means to be a leader.

Contents

Acknowledgment

Bhagyashree, my wife, for being with me and keeping me together.
Deepak Puranik, my brother, for inspiring me.
Kavan and Kunsh, my sons, for guiding me through the publishing process.

The quality of the *feathers on your wings* will decide how high and how long you will fly.

– Mama Eagle

Preface

The fact that you decided to read this book means that you are serious about your career and aspire to reach your full potential. Unfortunately, not many people try to unlock their potential. Many people have desires but fail to take any initiatives to fulfill those desires.

Congratulations!! You are already part of an exclusive club of aspirational youth.

Through this book, I have tried to share the wisdom that I have acquired during the 26 years of my professional career, on different continents, with different companies, and through challenging times. This wisdom has come through many experiences of failure and setbacks and some success stories. I am not a management guru or a research scholar. What I bring to you is the honesty of my wisdom and my pure experience. This book has been written with the desire that the new generation of business leaders should thrive and take on leadership roles in the business world for the greater good of society.

The purpose of this book is to bring to your attention some key topics that will impact your career and help you figure out what you can do about it. Knowledge of these key topics and their impact will make a difference in your career. Knowing them early in your career will help you grow faster, reach your full potential during your prime time, and avoid potential pitfalls.

This book is intended to make you curious so as to explore more about the topics of your interest. I encourage you to do more reading and research on topics of interest.

You are welcome to reach out to me through my email vivekpuranik72@gmail.com or on LinkedIn. It will be my pleasure to interact with you and exchange my thoughts. I will also look forward to your comments and suggestions for improvements in the next edition.

You will find that the language of this book is simple and colloquial. The idea is to reach as many youths as possible, globally.

I worked on this book with the hope that it will benefit the youth globally. I sincerely hope that you will benefit from my work and recommend my book to others to read and spread the good.

– Vivek Puranik
1655 Duncan Way
Streetsboro, Ohio – 44214
USA

Chapter 1: Know Yourself

Welcome to the Jungle

When you start your career as a young executive, just out of your college, you tend to define yourself with the credentials that you earned in college, your knowledge of the subjects that you studied, the sports that you are good at, your popularity in college, etc. You probably know yourself based on how your friends, teachers, and parents described you.

Good morning!! Wake up!! You will need to know more about yourself to ensure that you not only survive but thrive in this jungle of the business world. Welcome to the Jungle!!

Let me tell you a fact. You will grow old in this jungle and spend most of your productive life here. It is important that you have the right foundation, and you have a clear path to follow. For this, you will need to revisit yourself with a different perspective before you launch yourself.

The rules of this jungle are different, and you will need some additional skills to thrive. You will need to start from scratch, no matter how good or bad your past credentials are. Here, nobody cares what your friends or your parents think of you. You will have to make your own identity and sustain it for a lifetime.

Without knowing yourself and getting into the discipline of following ground rules that you set for yourself, you are not likely to go far or remain strong and happy.

If you are wondering why it is so important to know yourself at the beginning of your career, let me elaborate.

- If you have an opportunity to choose a job or a career path that matches your dominant character traits, knowing yourself will help you to adapt to the job faster and achieve success. If you are in a job that is not of your choice, then you are prepared to adapt better. Knowing yourself will help you to understand your weakness and susceptible areas, which you can work on to improve.

- Knowing yourself will also help you manage your professional relationships.
- Knowing yourself will help you lower the stress associated with ambition and allow you to grow faster.

There are several self-help books, many HR companies, and web services which can give you the professional help that you may need to know yourself better. However, I would recommend that you first introspect and find yourself.

Nobody knows you better than you can know yourself.

What do you play for?

"You play for respect and pride." - Rahul Dravid.

This inspirational quote by the legendary Indian cricketer largely sums up what young people today should focus on while building their careers.

Irrespective of where you work, what work you do, or what your position is in the company, without respect and pride your career would be worthless. What you really must earn is respect and be proud of the way you went about doing it.

The success, satisfaction, and longevity of your career will be decided by *the values* that you imbibe and demonstrate throughout your career.

The quality of *feathers on your wings* will decide how high and how long you fly.

The Values

"Values are those that do not change, ever."

Your strong beliefs may change when you see strong contrary proof or a convincing argument, but values do not change and should never be compromised.

You must have your own set of values which you would like to live by. Below I have listed my personal values which I have on my list. I highly recommend you keep them on your list too.

Integrity:

Be honest and have strong moral principles and be upright even when you are not being watched.

Intent:

Have a positive, unselfish, noble, and honest intent for your endeavors. The intent must be beyond yourself.

Capability:

Make yourself capable of the journey that you have taken up by seeking more knowledge, and working hard to develop the skills that are needed. Be in the right mental and physical zone to achieve your goals.

Results:

A result is an event or milestone and not the end of an endeavor and certainly not the end of everything.

Learn to accept results with humility, irrespective of whether they mean success or failure. You should only learn from the results and look forward to what you need to do to improve.

I am personally inspired by the sloka in *Bhagwat Gita* (A Hindu scripture that is part of the epic *Mahabharata*) which sums up why we do not "own" the results.

कर्मण्येवाधिकारस्ते मा फलेषु कदाचन
Karmanye Vadhikaraste ma phaleshu kadhachana.

The direct translation is - "Perform your duty but do not have any expectation of the fruits."

In this context, it means that we should perform our duties with integrity and good intent to the best of our capabilities and not worry about the results. To perform an action is under my control and I should focus on that. The results are not in my control, and I should learn to accept them with humility.

Motivation and Drive

Motivation and drive vary for everyone. Unfortunately, many do not care to understand what their personal motivations and drives are. A journey without motivation and drive can be compared to a reluctant traveler lost in the jungle. It is a painful and difficult journey.

As a young professional, you must discover your motivations and drives early on in your career. To help you understand them better, below is the best definition I could relate to -

"Motivation is that energy which makes you take initiatives and actions, to pursue goals and complete tasks. It's an inner push to act, create, and achieve. It is what pushes you to keep going on tasks and be persevering. Motivation is the 'why' behind everything you do."

Motivation improves self-confidence and drives you to do your best work to achieve your goals. It gives a purpose to your efforts and helps you remain balanced during setbacks and challenges. Staying motivated helps continual growth in your career.

"Drive" is the planned effort to achieve something.

If the benefit that you seek is intangible and is for self-improvement, the motivation is intrinsic. Intrinsic motivations stay with you for long and are characteristic of self-motivated people. An example would be that the motivation for reading self-help books can be to improve yourself.

If the benefit that you seek is tangible and helps you achieve some materialistic gratification, it's extrinsic motivation. These motivations are short-term in nature and end once you achieve the gratification that you were seeking. An example would be your motivation to use a particular airline to benefit from its loyalty program.

If you do not understand your motivations and drives, it will leave you confused in your career journey. You will lose focus and get distracted easily by external influences. In simple words, it would become a painful journey toward your goals.

Understand what motivates you and then pursue the goal. This will give you the grit and determination to pursue the goal no matter how much hardship you might have to endure or failures you may face.

To stay motivated throughout your career is difficult. There will be a low motivation period and you will need to pull yourself back up. You will need to recharge on the go.

To stay motivated, ensure the following:

Align your goals to your purpose: Keep reminding yourself of the purpose behind each goal that you are after. The purpose helps you with the motivation needed to keep putting in the best efforts in a sustained manner.

Develop a support circle: It is important to be surrounded by people who are optimistic and supportive of your endeavor to achieve your goals. You will need your circle to celebrate your successes with you and keep your energy levels high by reminding you how much you have accomplished and how the goal was achievable at times when you felt like you were losing motivation.

Celebrate even small successes: Celebration is a great positive emotion. You would want to experience this emotion as frequently as possible. This wanting to celebrate will help keep you motivated.

Celebrate even the small accomplishments and all milestones along your path. This gives you a sense of accomplishment and confidence that you are on the right path.

Let your goals be SMART: Choose your goals wisely. Consider what you want to accomplish and why. Analyze the pros and cons. Structure your goals to be SMART.

S - Specific. Well-defined goals with the who, what, where, when, and why of your tasks.

M – Measurable. Define a key indicator that will help you decide if a goal is reached.

A – Achievable – Create goals that are achievable considering the skills and resources that you have.

R – Relevant. Let the goals be as true to reality as possible.

T – Time-bound. Let the goals have a deadline for you to achieve.

Are you an Extrovert or an Introvert?

Understand your personality. There is nothing wrong if you are an introvert, and nothing great if you are an extrovert. Success is not guaranteed if you are either. Success rather has a higher possibility if you know what you are, and then adapt to what is needed by acquiring the skill gaps you have.

Choose a career path that will suit your personality trait. This is a good approach toward success.

While it is true that the chances of extroverts rising to the top is higher, a research published in Harvard Business Review, by Adam Grant, Francesca Gino, and David Hofmann suggests that an introvert can make a better boss when leading proactive employees.

Introverts, generally tend to:

- Enjoy spending time alone.
- Think before speaking or acting.
- Are generally reserved.
- Prefer working independently rather than in a team.

Extroverts, generally tend to:

- Gain energy in a social situation.
- Can make quick decisions.
- Are outgoing.
- Like working in a team.

If you have more traits of an extrovert, you will adapt with more ease to jobs where you will need to be more outgoing and have interactions with people that you may not know. Examples are event management, sales, customer service, etc.

If you are an introvert and end up in jobs that need the traits of an extrovert, you will need to work on some traits and adapt, and vice versa. This is the advantage of knowing yourself. Since you know your personality better, you will know the traits that you are weak in, and you will work harder on them. Thus, understanding your personality will give you confidence and a path for improvement.

Irrespective of what management gurus and research will tell you, being an introvert or extrovert is situational. You can adapt to become one or the other if needed. I would say that both these terms are highly overrated.

It is okay if you are an introvert or an extrovert, the best part is that you know it and you can adapt better.

My Notes:

Name:

Date:

A. My Values:

1.
2.
3.
4.

B. I am an____________________ (Introvert / Extrovert)

C. What motivates me?

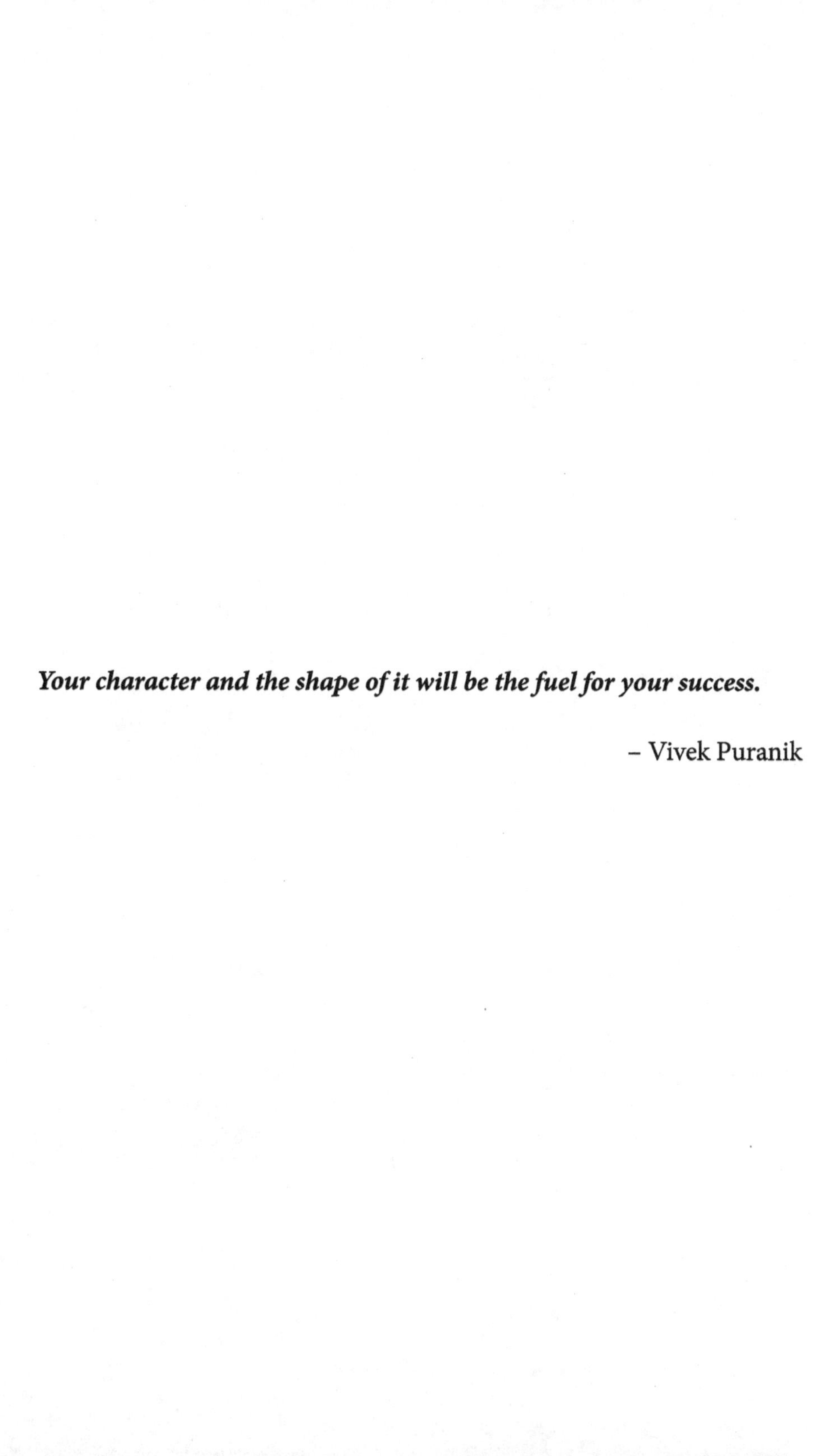

Your character and the shape of it will be the fuel for your success.

– Vivek Puranik

Chapter 2: Know Your Business World

Know Your Company

The new recruits in the company tend to believe that they know about the company they work for, based on what information is available in public domains. I do not blame them for their ignorance, but reading what is written, is not "knowing." You will need to go beyond that. You will need to understand the business.

Understanding the business, in simple terms, means that you must know how your company is making money (generating profits).

Irrespective of your role or your position in the organization's structure, you must understand the business of your company. Having a good understanding of business will help you to have a better perspective of your role and understand what is expected from you in terms of your contribution to either creating, selling, or servicing the product that your company makes.

To understand your company better, you will need to know the following –

- Know your products.
- Know your customers.
- Know your market.

Know Your Product

The product is the one that your company sells to generate income, primarily. These products can be physical or virtual. They can be services or value additions.

You must know the products well. It is a bare minimum requirement that you understand the product applications, its limitations, and detailed specifications. Well, this is what everyone in your company will possibly know. You will need to go beyond this, fly high and get a bird eye view and know more about your product.

How is the product generated/manufactured?
You must understand the manufacturing process and key inputs that go into making the product. It can be raw materials, technology, the skills of technicians, or special processes. Understand the stages of the manufacturing process and how they are adding value to the product.

Who is making the product?
You must know about the people behind the creation of the product. These people can be from various departments in your company like R&D, engineering, production, quality, and logistics, etc. Interact with these people to know the product creation process.

Where is the product made?
The final product generally is an assembly of various subcomponents or subsystems. There will be multiple value-adding processes that need to be completed before the final product is ready to be sold to the customers. There are likely to be multiple locations involved in making the products

and their subcomponents. Understand where the subcomponents are added and where and what kind of value addition is done in the manufacturing process.

How is the supply chain structured?

The efficiency of the supply chain is the key differentiating factor for the competing companies. Understand the supply chain structure. Have knowledge about the sourcing of key raw materials and sub-vendors that are part of the value stream.

How is the product delivered to customers?

Packing and delivery performance are customer experience parameters. They give an opportunity to impress your customer and add to his good experience with your product, even before he starts using the product. Understand how it is packed and why. Understand if the finished product has any special storage needs. Know other logistical information to understand how your company is ensuring that it meets the customer expectations of the physical delivery of the product.

What are the unique features of your product (USP – Unique Selling Proposition)?

You must know what it is that makes your customers choose to buy your product regularly.

Know Your Customers

Customers are the ones who are paying for the purchase of your product or service.

The company exists because of the customers and not the other way round. Customers generally have a choice. The value proposition of your product makes your customers choose your product over those of your competitors.

Irrespective of the role and position in the organization, everyone in the company gets paid because your customers are paying for your products.

Any company which is not customer-centric in its approach will cease to exist sooner rather than later. Having a customer-centric mindset is a key growth factor in your career.

Know the following about your customers -

1. Who are the **top 10 customers** of your company?
2. What is the **profile** of these top customers? Are they individual buyers or corporate buyers? What is their business?
3. What is the **value addition** that your product provides to your customer's business and how vital is it?
4. Are you the **sole supplier** of this product or does your customer have multiple sources i.e., are they also buying from your competitor?
5. Why are your customers buying from your company? How do your customers evaluate your company? What are the **top 4 deliverables** that are most important to your customer?
    - Price
    - On-time delivery
    - Quality

- Safety
- Reliability
- Compliance
- Innovation
- Sustainability
- Packing

6. **What is the organizational structure** of your customer organization?
7. **Who are the key decision-makers** in the customers' organization?
8. How **digitally evolved** are your customers?
9. What are the **synergies** between your company and the customers' business?
10. How is the **relationship** of your company with your customers?

Know Your Markets

The market for your products is the space where there is a potential chance, however small, to sell the product directly or indirectly.

Know the following about your markets -

1. What is the **total size** of the market for your product, in terms of units and value of sales?
2. What is the **addressable market** for your products? Addressable by product limitations, policy, and reach to the market.
3. What is the **market share** of your company?
4. Who are your **major competitors** and what are their shares in the market?
5. What is the nature of the **market economy**?

Perfect Competition: This type of market has many different buyers and sellers. No buyer or seller can influence the market price because buyers and sellers will have infinite alternatives.

Monopoly: This type of market has only one producer who can influence the price to its benefit; however, the revenue will be limited by the ability or willingness of the customer to pay the price.

Oligopoly: This type of market has a handful of dominant producers and without diligent government regulations, the oligopoly market will act like a monopoly market with the producers forming a cartel to dictate the prices in the market.

Monopolistic Competition: In this market type, there are numerous buyers and sellers but each one is sufficiently differentiated from the other and hence some can charge a greater price than the other, which will not be the case in a perfect competition market.

Monopsony: In this market type, there are multiple sellers and a single buyer, which gives significant power to the buyer in determining the prices.

Understand **market segmentation** and how it affects your product. Popularly, markets are segmented based on -

- Demographic segmentation
- Geographic segmentation
- Firmographic segmentation
- Psychographic segmentation
- Behavioral segmentation

There can be other segmentations based on the industry and the locations of the business.

Understand the **market trends** of the past and the future.

Understand how the market has grown in the past and at what pace. The compound annual growth rate (CAGR) can be one of the key indicators of the market growth pace.

Understand what are the "**market drivers**" in each category below -

- Social and behavioral drivers
- Economics and policy drivers
- Technology drivers
- Resources drivers

Understand the **sensitivity of market growth** with economic fundamentals.

- What happens if inflation increases?
- What happens when interest rates fall?
- How do foreign exchange rates affect the market?
- Which economic policy of the government can affect the market?

Understand **market risks**. The risks are always hidden in the drivers and opportunities. Hence the risk can again be classified into the following groups -

- Social and behavioral risks
- Economics and policy risks
- Technology risks
- Resources risks

Know the Buying Process

Business is about selling and buying. Selling and buying are two faces of the same coin. Knowing your buyer and the buying process will increase your business acumen.

You must have knowledge of the following about your buyer/customer -

- The buying process of the buyer.
- The people involved in the process and their roles.
- The buyer's need.
- The present mental state of the buyer in the task of buying.
- The buyer's mental approach towards the buying task.
- The buyer's understanding of the solution available.
- The buyer's understanding of the market and competition.
- The buyer's budget.

The buyer's preferences if any. Buyers may have preferences for very vague reasons that you may not appreciate.

You need to remember that every buyer has a specific need. The objective of the buyer is to delight their internal and external stakeholders. There is a very strong reason for you being allowed to approach him.

You must know the **status of your buyer's buying process** and the approach that he would take in the buying process. Evaluate and understand the current stage of your buyer and then design your approach to engage with him accordingly. Every buyer will pass through the following stages in his buying process -

- The buyer is happy or unaware of the options available.
- The buyer is aware that a change is possible or needed.

- The buyer has a definite desire to change.
- The buyer is assessing the need.
- The buyer is defining the needs.
- The buyer is in the process of market research/evaluating the options.
- The buyer is in the process of negotiations.
- The buyer has made the decision to order.
- The buyer is in the process of evaluating the decision.

If the buying process is not followed stage-wise, post-sale dissonance is likely. This means that the buyer will question his own decision of buying. This will lead to an inefficient selling and buying process.

Knowledge of the buying process is important for people both in buying and selling roles.

Know the Technology

The efficient use of technology for optimizing business results is one of the strategic differentiators for competing companies. Hence, being in sync with the current technology is a key requirement.

The knowledge of the core technical subjects that you study in college is no longer enough for you to progress in your career or compete with your peers. You will need to develop the ability to use computer-based technology to complete different tasks efficiently. It would be highly beneficial if you invested to train yourself in these skills on priority and update and upgrade as needed.

The basic expectation on any job these days is –

- Computer literacy
- Skills to navigate the web
- Database management
- Computation software like Excel
- Communication via email and the use of social media
- Skills to handle calls over the computer
- Presentation skills on PowerPoint etc.
- Word processing skills
- Business communication skills

Apart from the above basic skills, you must be skilled in specific software or applications related to your core area of expertise. Examples of application software can be Microsoft Projects for project management professionals.

S.W.O.T Analysis

SWOT analysis is a very effective tool to help you see how your company stands out, the vulnerability it faces, and what opportunities it has in the marketplace.

S.W.O.T is an abbreviation for -

S - Strengths
W - Weakness
O - Opportunities
T - Threats

It is widely used as a key tool in most corporations as part of strategy building. It is very effective and easy to use. The SWOT analysis helps to bring perspective to the company's strengths and weaknesses and see how they contribute to opportunities and risks. The purpose is to develop a strategic action plan to maximize these opportunities and minimize the risks.

Tips to make SWOT more effective –

- Do a SWOT analysis in two sets.
    1. Looking internally
    2. Looking from the outside, from your customer's perspective.
- Compare both the SWOTs and note down the differences. These gaps are the ones that you will need to analyze further and develop a strategic action plan to execute it.

- Do not list your feelings or wishes in the SWOT chart; be as honest as practically possible; be critical and blunt to state the facts. Do not sugar-quote the facts to make them look good. **The bad needs to sound bad.**
- For every action that you feel needs to be on the chart, state the impact on the business. If the impact is not quantifiable, use your best estimate.
- Based on the impact, categorize them into different buckets like "critical," "important," and "watch out." The action plan for execution needs to be prioritized based on whether it is in a critical, important, or watch-out stage.

The objective of the action plan needs to be to –

- Convert the strengths to generate more business and maximize the impact.
- Work on the opportunities to build midterm and long-term business prospects.
- Analyze the risks due to the weaknesses and fix them. Plan to minimize the negative impact.
- Monitor the threats and work to eliminate them based on how "clear and present" they are.

SWOT needs to be done at least twice a year. Every new SWOT needs to be compared with the previous one to check for the progress being made and evaluate if the execution of the action plan from last time is having its impact already.

SWOT for Career Growth

SWOT analysis is very helpful for individual development plans within your organization.

Once you understand the weakness of your company and the threats that can impact the business, you will know the skill sets that your company will need to overcome these weaknesses and threats. You can start to acquire the skill sets which will line you up for growth with your organization.

My Notes:

Date:

3 things I want to know more about my company.

1.

2.

3.

3 things I want to know more about my market.

1.

2.

3.

3 things I want to know more about my product.

1.

2.

3.

3 things I want to know more about technology.

1.

2.

3.

My Notes:

SWOT for my company -

Strengths:	Weaknesses:
1.	1.
2.	2.
3.	3.
Opportunities:	**Threats:**
1.	1.
2.	2.
3.	3.

My Notes:

What are the skills that my company will need, in the near future and long-term, to maximize the opportunities and minimize the threats?

1.
2.
3.

How will I acquire these skills?

1.
2.
3.

Chapter 3: The Right Approach for a Successful Career

I have wings, I will fly.....
I will fly high.
– Baby Eagle

Prepare

'Preparations' are the roots of your tree of success.

Preparation does not guarantee your success but increases the chances of success exponentially. You must start with mental preparation and commit to being organized and disciplined. Preparation for the next step should become part of your daily routine.

When you start to prepare, you will think of the task ahead of you. This means that you will be thinking of the objectives, obstacles, execution, and intended impact related to the task that you are preparing for. Preparations have a great effect on execution. You will sail through the execution. Good preparation also means that you will find it difficult to start till you are ready. Knowing that you are not ready is already a great start and is a result of your effective preparation process.

Some key points to consider when you start preparing are –

- Check on the expected deliverables. What you want to achieve through the task that you are preparing for.
- Check what information, skills, and tools would be needed to deliver. If you need to collaborate with your colleagues, reach out early, and give sufficient time to them to give you quality input.
- Plan to complete your task in advance as well to have some time to check, and reflect, for peer consultation.

Practice

Practice takes you closer to success … consistently.

Learning something new is challenging. It can be hard and exhausting at times. Getting good at a new skill is only possible through practice. You can never learn how to swim by reading about it. Knowing how to do a task is not the same as doing the task yourself. Most people are reluctant to practice. These are the people who normally are overshadowed by the few people who opt to practice. The reason for avoiding practice can be overconfidence, ego, laziness, lack of commitment, or sheer foolishness.

Those few who practice have the best chance to reach their full potential. It is certainly not enough if you just grasp the concept or idea, it is required to acquire the skills to execute. These skills can be mastered only through practice.

Your company would train you in new skills or coach you on key behaviors. Unless you follow up the training and coaching with consistent practice, all the time and other resources invested in you are a waste. By not practicing, you are hurting your chances of reaching your full potential in your career.

You will need practice to move from **"knowing"** something to **"I can manage"** to **"I am pretty good at it"** to **"I am an expert."** Learn to embrace the discomfort of being a beginner. Embrace success.

Practice -

- provides you with career boosters.
- helps you polish your skills.
- helps you gain confidence.
- helps you learn to improvise.
- helps you bounce back after a failure.
- helps you be ready to learn new things.

Reflect

Reflecting rationalizes your preparation and practice, and keeps you on the path of continuous success.

Make it a daily routine to reflect on what and how you did today and if there was anything that you could do to improve if you had to do the same tomorrow. This is a life skill. Reflecting is a very powerful tool. It will help to get a perspective of what has happened. It will also help you cool your nerves by reducing anxiety. Reflecting will help you analyze yourself with an optimistic mindset.

Make sure that you are **balanced** when you reflect, without being very hard on yourself. Also, do not be overconfident.

Look at **things that you can control,** and at the same time avoid blaming others.

Reflect on the **efforts and preparation** that you made rather than on the results achieved.

Measure yourself based on your **own expectations** rather than those of others.

Try to find at least one thing that you could have **done better**. Keep notes on what you reflect upon and your observations.

Be Assertive

The assertive approach differentiates a leader from the rest.

Being assertive means being able to stand up for your own or other peoples' rights calmly and positively without being aggressive, and without passively accepting wrong.

Aggression and assertion are commonly mistaken for each other. Being aggressive is not the same as being assertive.

Some simple steps to start practicing assertiveness are –

- Express yourself clearly and confidently.
- Maintain eye contact when communicating.
- Learn to say "no" in a calm but firm way.
- Rather than aiming to win all the time, learn to express your needs.

Assertiveness will help -

- To create honest relationships.
- To improve decision-making skills.
- To understand and recognize your own feelings.

Being assertive will help you earn respect from others. You will create more winning situations and gain self-confidence. Your self-esteem will be high.

Assertiveness will help you get better opportunities to grow in leadership roles.

Structured Approach

A structured approach will keep you ahead in the race for career endurance.

Look back and see how you used to react earlier when a new task was given to you.

How did you approach the task?
Did you rush with excitement?
Were you overwhelmed?
Did you go numb and dumb?
Did you try to run away?
Did you wish you had received a different task?
Is it a combination of some of the above or all the above?

If your answer is any, or all of the above, don't be too hard on yourself. Most of us have never been trained to approach a task or a challenge in a structured way. We are expected to 'figure it out' ourselves.

A few people who are naturally structured or a handful who figure it out themselves stand out in their careers, leaving others to wonder how these guys managed to climb the corporate ladder faster.

There are several benefits of having a structured approach.

- With a structured approach, you are **less stressed.**
- With a structured approach, you are **in control** of the "known" and **not fearful** of the "unknown."
- With a structured approach, the probability of **success is higher.**

- With a structured approach, **progress is measured** and visible to you and your organization.
- With a structured approach, **success is seen as a product of sustained effort** and not a fluke or a last-minute push.
- With a structured approach, you will have a lot of **data points for learning** even if you fail. You have a trail to track.
- With a structured approach, you can fully **comprehend the contribution** (or otherwise) of all the team members and the support (or otherwise) of your bosses.
- With a structured approach, the **results can be replicated** with relative ease.
- Your company leadership **will have higher confidence** in you to execute missions and critical assignments for the company.

You can develop a structured approach by following a few simple steps when you are assigned a task.

1. **Know** your task.
2. **Analyze** your task.
3. **Plan** your task.
4. **Execute** your task.

Know the Task

Understand the task as clearly as possible. Start with answers to the following questions -

- What is the objective of the task and what is to be **achieved?**
- What is the **value** of this task for the stakeholders and for me?
- What are the **"Key Performance Indicators"** (KPI) that would define the success of this task?
- Is this a subtask of a bigger task? How are they **connected?**
- What is the level of **criticality** of the task for your team and for your company?
- Who is your sponsor and who are the key stakeholders?
- How will a positive result or a negative result affect your sponsor and the key stakeholders?

Analyze the task

During the analyzing phase, ask the following questions -

- What are the **skills** that would be critical to complete this task successfully?
- **Do I have** the skills needed to complete the task successfully?
- What are the **gaps?** How do you plan to fill the gaps in the skill set? Will you learn? Will you hire? Will you ask for help?
- What **resources** will you need to complete the task successfully? Do you have them? Where will you get them?
- What is the **cost** of these resources?
- Have I listed all the **assumptions** being made and are the stakeholders aware of the assumptions being made?
- What are the **risks** (internal and external)? How severe are they? What is the probability of these risks? (Severity X probability gives you the impact of the risk. Make sure that you have a mitigation plan for high-impact risks.

Plan the task

After you have answers to the questions in the analyzing phase, put together the plan on paper. Some key points that you must address during the planning phase are –

- Allocate the resources you have and use your skillset to ensure that the task is completed before the deadline.
- Your plan must have well-defined milestones to check how much is achieved and what is achieved.
- Your plan must be realistic and achievable to the best of your knowledge and abilities.
- Allocate buffer time for high-risk tasks, assuming anything that can go wrong will go wrong.
- Share the plan with your sponsor, other team members, and stakeholders and ask for feedback.

There are several tools available to help you plan your task/project. An example is MS Projects. You can easily get trained through videos or by enrolling in courses on digital for no expense or very little investment. It will be worth your time and investment.

Most organizations today expect that all the key challenges and developments get handled like a project. Project management is one of the key skills that the organization will expect you to possess.

Execute the task

Execution is the most important and difficult part of the entire process of being structured.

Execution is about putting your resources into action to ensure that the deliverables for the project/task milestones are always on track.

Collaboration and communication are the keys to success during execution.

Follow up for the input that you will need from others, in and outside your team. Check periodically to ensure that all activities that are being done by others are on track. Ask them to raise "red flags" as and when they see a risk, and not wait for the follow-up.

It is very effective to have regular focused meetings of short durations for following up and tracking.

Communicate the progress of the task to the sponsor and the stakeholders regularly. This can be done either by setting up regular progress meetings or reports. Communication must be transparent, irrespective of whether you think you have good news or bad news to communicate.

When there is a setback in the execution or the progress is not as per the plan, communicate the action plan to catch up and highlight the impact of the delay on the overall task. List the learnings.

Communicate the learnings you can take from the setbacks or failures that you have had.

Communicate about how you have used the learnings from the past to **prevent some of the likely pitfalls**, which otherwise could have had a negative impact.

Use past learnings to have a positive impact on results. **Calibrate and adjust** plans as you go along, with a focus on the deliverables. Communicate all changes.

Make celebrations a key part of the execution. Celebrate with your team, not only when you complete the task but also celebrate every milestone achieved and every small success that is important for the task and team.

Enjoy your journey, rest awhile at your destination, and start a new one. There is no stopping a structured effort.

"Being structured is your ladder to the moon. You will still need to climb it though."

Eye for Detail

Every person is different by nature. The level with which each person gets into detail is different.

If you are a person who likes to get into detail naturally, it's a blessing. Eye for detail is very impactful for your career.

- Eye for detail will make you more curious and being **curious** will help you **learn more and learn faster**.
- Eye for detail means you care for the quality **of information** you get and pass on.
- Eye for detail is a **key leadership quality** which will get you more challenging tasks with higher responsibility. This means an opportunity to grow faster.

In the context of the task you perform, an eye for details can –

- Help reduce errors.
- Increase efficiency.
- Enhance the final product.

If you are not a person who has an eye for detail naturally, you can practice and adapt to be one.

Some simple ways to develop an eye for detail are –

- Prepare and research before you begin.
- Have a checklist to track your tasks and progress.
- Do not rush or do any last-minute work.
- Review your work before marking it complete.
- Use the four eyes practice where you can ask another person to check your work before marking it complete.

Understand the frequent and common mistakes you make during a task. Go slow on them.

Career caution: If you are not a person who has an eye for detail and if you cannot invest in developing this skill, you must avoid careers in accounting, finance, auditing, and quality.

Career Plan: One Step at a Time

One step at a time approach helps you form a very strong foundation for your skills and ensures sustained growth for your career. It also ensures that you have a healthy work-life balance.

It is natural for you to rush when you see an open space in front of you. You will be tempted to grab the opportunity that has been presented to you. You will rush without analyzing if it is in line with what you want to achieve, in the mid and long-term.

- Do not rush in blind faith. When exciting opportunities come to you, pause, evaluate, and then take an **informed decision**.
- Have a career plan outlook for the next 3 years.
- Define where you would like to reach with respect to position, responsibility, and monetary compensation in the near future. Based on where you need to go, you will need to decide the direction and the skill sets that you will need to acquire and the time frame to do so. Ensure that you have time to continue your hobby and manage a healthy work-life balance. Running in the wrong direction can slow you down in the long run and can be a reason for stress.

Build Trust Through Transparency

Trust is like a house of cards. It takes a lot of effort and time to build one, but it can be destroyed with little effort.

In the corporate world, one of the most effective ways to build trust with your peers and higher up is through transparency. Clear communication and a structured approach will help you get the trust of senior leadership. Having a professional relationship with your leadership, based on trust, will boost your growth prospects. Building trust through transparency is very helpful, especially during the beginning of your career and with new bosses, new leaders, or new customers.

Following a structured approach is key. Some tips to display transparency in your work are -

- Learn to **communicate the "Bad news."** Keep all stakeholders updated on all the relevant information that they need to know.
- If you see any **risks** in the tasks assigned to you, with respect to completion dates or any other KPIs, **communicate** them as soon as you can.
- If you want a **decision, ask for it**. If the decision is time sensitive, follow up regularly with the decision-makers.
- **Take decisions** and inform everyone about all the decisions that you have taken. Share the background work that you did to arrive at a decision. Clearly state all the assumptions you made in taking a business decision and get them validated.

- If you find any **issues or mistakes** in already submitted work, **inform** stakeholders along with the correction, impact, and information about what you will do to make sure this mistake is not repeated in future tasks.

Trust is the key to team success. In the professional world, trust does not come with relations or positions. Trust can be built with sustained efforts and discipline.

Manage workplace pressure

Pressure is unavoidable in the workplace. You will be under pressure all the time during your career. This is a fact. You may feel greater pressure if you are ambitious and competitive. You must find ways to manage and handle the pressure.

Allowing the pressure to get to you can have multiple effects not only on your career but also on your health and your family life. It can throw your work-life balance off the track and increase your stress levels, which can be harmful in the long run.

A structured approach is an excellent tool to manage pressure. Some tips to manage pressure better are mentioned below -

1. Take on what you can handle and deliver with quality and on time. Many times, during the early part of your career, it is natural to get ove-excited and underestimate the complexities of the new tasks that are assigned to you, or to volunteer to take up new tasks due to over-enthusiasm.

2. Know the deliverables of the project before you take it. It is also true that in many cases, the specifics of the deliverable are not spelled out in detail and hence it is more important that you understand what is to be delivered, when, and with what level of quality. It is never about just completing the task or being part of it. It is about the Key Performance Indicators (KPIs) of the deliverables. If you understand the KPI of each new task, you will know how much you can deliver without excess pressure.

3. Learn to say no. The weak experience maximum pressure. In a competitive work environment, the weak get exposed and thus are vulnerable to maximum pressure. Learning to say "no" is a key personality trait that you will need to develop. You will need to understand that you cannot always make all the people happy. Learning to say no has a positive effect too. You will be looked at as a person who is assertive and who knows what he is doing. Initially, though, some eyebrows will be raised, and some egos hurt. Soon you will be respected and valued as a reliable person.

4. Manage expectations. Reputation and expectations can be a major cause of pressure and stress. Learn to be tactful and diplomatic when committing. Do not compete on committing, compete on delivering. Promise less than what you can deliver and deliver more than what you promise. The other way round can be very stressful and will put your career under pressure.

5. Focus on the process rather than on the results. Many schools of philosophy tell us to disassociate from the results. Famously, in *Bhagwat Geeta,* the ancient Hindu text, it is said that we are only obliged to put in the right efforts and are not responsible for or own the results of these efforts, irrespective of whether the results are good or bad.

This can be a bit confusing and contradictory to what the corporate industry will expect from you starting day one. You are expected to be "result oriented."

You may often hear your boss say, "All that I care about is the results." This can cause a lot of stress and pressure for the teams and individuals involved.

The pressure of results can be managed if you understand and believe that results are the output of your process and if the process is not robust and not followed meticulously, there is no way that you will be able to get consistent and predictable results.

6. Philosophy of hard work: The basis for the pressure or the stress is not the work itself, it is you and your ability to manage it. Hence, the reason for pressure and stress can only be you and nothing else. To manage pressure or stress, it is not only enough to have good processes or work instructions at your workplace, but also how you approach your work challenges as an individual.

Some questions to consider to manage pressure better are –

- What is my philosophy towards hard work? How am I motivated to direct my efforts in the right direction to achieve the results?
- How disciplined am I in following the process that I set for myself?
- How do I handle the feedback and make changes in the process for better results?

7. **Ask for help**. Asking for help when needed, and at the right time, is never a sign of weakness. Rather, it's a sign of your inner strength. It helps you to reduce the pressure build-up. The leaders will see you as a person who reaches out and collaborates to achieve results. This is a key trait of successful future leaders, which you aspire to be.

8. **Healthy work-life balance** plays a big role in managing work-related pressure. You can only minimize the pressure and manage it but cannot avoid it. You will need to have your own ways of managing the pressure and stress to ensure that it does not affect your life in general. The way to manage stress can be very personal and hence everyone will have his own way to do so. Some of the ways can be -

- Exercise/Practice Yoga/Run/Walk
- Pranayama/Breathing exercise
- Develop a hobby
- Spend quality time with your family/friends
- Play sports
- Learn to switch off.
- Keep digital blackout days
- Take planned vacations

Your ability to manage high-pressure situations will help you enjoy the situation and will soon make you one of the most reliable and best leaders, who can manage any crisis for the company.

9. **Enjoy the challenge:** Enjoy the challenges that come your way. Being structured will help you enjoy any new challenge that comes your way, both professional and personal.

Some key reminders are –

- Be thorough in the process.
- Prepare well.
- Be well-informed.
- Be objective oriented.
- Be flexible to reach a solution.
- Be disciplined.

Chapter 4: Essential Skills to Power Your Career to the Next Level

Presentation and Reports

Presentations are the most effective means to convey information to a target audience with a specific purpose. The purpose can be to inform, present a new idea, share findings, persuade, motivate, or inspire.

The presentation method and delivery are as important as the content itself. Effective presentation is a skill that needs to be practiced and developed.

You must acknowledge the difference between a report and a presentation.

A report normally is an elaborate and meticulous account of information on a particular topic. The report will normally have a defined structure and is expected to have some amount of research done to get the information needed. Reports are normally always focused on the topic.

Presentations are normally done to summarize the reports and highlight the key takeaways for decision-making or for developing actionable agendas. It's a tool to skim your report and highlight what is relevant to the target audience.

Let me clarify with an example. Let us assume that you and your team have made a report on a new product development that has detailed data analysis, calculations, and assumptions incorporated. However, if you are scheduled to have a discussion with the finance team, you may decide to make a presentation that would include only the topics of interest to the target audience. In this case, most likely it would be about product profitability. From the several hundred pages of your report, you will make a presentation of a few slides that will address topics of interest like product costs, cost assumptions, maximum and minimum salable prices, risks, etc. Of course, you can refer to the report if more detailed information is required by the audience.

There are several articles available on the web on how to make an effective presentation, which you can read and practice for yourself.

Given below are some basic tips to prepare a presentation -

Developing the presentation content

Know your audience. Know, in advance, who your audience is. The corporate positions, designations, hierarchy, and other key stakeholders. It is obvious that the presentation that you would develop for senior leadership will be different from the one that you would make for the junior managers.

Understand the context of the presentation. It is important to understand the objective of the presentation. The objective can be to make a decision, get a direction, just plain information on progress, defend a decision, support an investigation, etc. The content, flow, and impact must be different based on the context of the presentation.

Use logic and flow. The presentation should be a flow of logic that the target audience should be able to relate to and easily understand.

Message. Every slide must have a message for your audience. Any slide without a message is a waste of time and needs to be only on your backup.

Expect and anticipate questions. Be ready to deep dive when needed and be familiar with the backup and reference material. Roleplay is of great help while preparing for these questions. The fact that you had anticipated a particular question and are prepared to answer it gives a lot of confidence to the stakeholders.

Summarize the important and relevant assumptions and highlight the work-in-progress areas.

Confirmed and correct information. Ensure that only the correct information is presented in very simple language, irrespective of whether it is good news or bad news. Ensure that you have confirmed and cross-checked all the information that is being fed to you before you put it in the presentation.

Below are some general tips on presentation slides -

- Always use your company's standard **template** slide for all your professional presentations.
- Ideally, an effective presentation should not have more than **10 to 15 slides.**
- The first slide after the agenda slide must **focus** on why this presentation is happening and what we need to achieve by the end of this presentation.
- The last slide has the **summary** of the key takeaway with the conclusion. This slide should remain with the audience even after the presentation.
- The slides should have as **little text** as possible and more relevant pictures.
- The **font** should be readable and consistent.
- No more than **3 points** need to be highlighted per slide.
- Each slide should have a **key takeaway** at the bottom of the slide, adequately highlighted.
- **Avoid using animations/effects/ sounds** in corporate presentations. They are only for kids.

Delivery of presentation:

Practice your presentation. Even the best presenters fail without sufficient practice.

Acknowledge your audience before you start with eye contact and try to maintain optimum eye contact with your audience.

Speak slowly and clearly; make sure you are understood.

Do not rush through any slide but make sure you respect the time allocated for your presentation.

Time management is vital for effective presentation.

Clarify misunderstandings as soon as you feel there are any. Be attentive to the words you use.

Ask for help when needed. Keep your team and backup data handy for help.

Never give false information or set high expectations just to please your audience.

Interact with your audience after the presentation and ask for feedback.

Avoid using jargon or casual language. Use simple language with correct grammar irrespective of the language you want to use for the presentation.

Use pictures to convey your message. This will be very effective if your audience is of different cultural backgrounds, or ethnicity or is not fully conversant in the language of your presentation.

Be **culturally sensitive** and avoid being offensive intentionally or unintentionally.

Presenting to Senior Management

Presenting to senior management can be challenging and stressful if preparation is not adequate. The time value of your audience will be very high, and the attention span of your audience is likely to be very limited. Not to underestimate the influence of political and ego undercurrents that will present itself when multiple senior managers are in one room. Presentation for senior management demands additional preparations.

- Keep a shorter version of your presentation ready as plan B. You may have to use this if the time allotted to you gets cut down.
- Be ready to facilitate a discussion among the decision-makers without being political. Present facts and speak your mind.
- If all the key decision makers are not present, ask the senior person if the quorum is enough to take the decision before starting the presentation.
- If the audience is distracted and is not attentive, stop the presentation to check if the topics are important for all.
- If the key decision maker is leaving before the end of the presentation, check with him if the rest can make a decision.
- Be ready to improvise when needed. If the topics change during the discussion, diplomatically request a re-focus on the subject.

Basic knowledge of finance

Business is **"everything about money."** Hence if you are part of any business and want to contribute to its growth and grow professionally with your business, you must have a basic knowledge of finance.

A basic knowledge of finance will help you understand and analyze the business and provide you with foresight on solutions for business challenges.

- A basic knowledge of finance will help you analyze the **financial health** of an organization. You can learn to read and analyze -
  - Profit and loss statements
  - Cash flow statements
  - Balance sheets.

This financial acumen will help you analyze the **reasons behind the financial performance of the company**.

Let me clarify with an example. The financial performance of the company is showing a loss in profits v/s the previous year's results. The sales have improved by 20% v/s the previous year. The profit and loss account will give you information if any or all of the reasons listed below are the reasons for the abnormal financial results.

- Higher direct material/labor costs
- Higher fixed cost
- Loss of volumes
- Price erosion, etc.

You can work on the reasons to fix the issue to understand the following -

- You will understand the **cash position** of your company and the importance of making your customers pay on time as agreed.

- You will understand how every small saving due to continuous improvements and process orientation, safety, inspections, etc. adds up to **generating more money** and better results.
- You will get a **better perspective of your role in the organization** w.r.t your contribution to profit generation for your organization.

Young executives and managers with a better understanding of financial concepts gain a lot of soft power in the organization.

Young leaders with a better understanding of finance will naturally get more responsibility considering that money is the most important resource of any organization. Profits and cash are the key parameters on which the company will be judged by investors and owners.

Where to start?

First, you need to have the mindset that finance is common sense and not quantum physics.

- Enroll for a course that is available online, in-person, as part of higher studies.
- There are many books and YouTube videos that are available on the internet that you can refer to.
- Take the help of mentors or senior finance executives in your company.
- "Finance for non-finance professionals" certificate course is available online and in person.
- Take an internship with the financial department to spend extra hours with your finance department.

"You can leave the finance to experts only when you understand it."

1:1 Meetings

1:1 A meeting is a periodic, focused meeting between two people to review all topics of business and personal development.

You must proactively schedule regular 1:1 meetings with your manager. These meetings need to be periodic, bi-weekly. The agenda of the meeting should be designed in such a way that you use this exclusive time with your boss to –

- Update on the progress of various tasks.
- Get directions.
- Get decisions.
- Check for his/her inputs.
- Ask for feedback.

Ensure that you maintain the minutes of the meeting and share them with your manager after the meeting. Managers tend to have selective memory syndrome!

These meetings are extremely helpful to avoid surprises. This will help you to connect better with your manager. Use these meetings to develop a rapport with your manager. This is also a good time to share common interests beyond work.

Ensure that your subordinates have a 1:1 meeting with you, where you review all the above points, now as a manager.

Be "P.E.R.F.E.C.T."

Positive personality traits are key career drivers for young executives and managers. Personality development should be part of the individual development plan of all young executives.

Key personality traits you must acquire and improve are listed below.
P - Practical: Be practical in your approach, behavior, and commitments and demonstrate assertive behavior.

E - Excellent Communicator: Strive to become an excellent communicator. This means you need to -

1. Be a good listener.
2. Be always approachable.
3. Make customized presentations to reach specific people.
4. Show genuine interest.
5. Speak effectively and to the point.
6. Be punctual.
7. Be friendly and display a good sense of humor.

R-Ready: Be ready to recognize the change early and adapt to the situation to manage the change. Be ready to change your own mindset and that of your teams and customers as well, if required.

F-Focus: Be focused on the objectives that need to be achieved. Focus also means sacrificing that which is not your priority.

E-Energy Levels: Stay high on energy. Make deliberate attempts to radiate energy to the people around you. Do not procrastinate.

C-Customer centric: Constantly focus on delighting your customers, both internally and externally. There is no better way to grow in your career.

T-Trustworthy: Be trustworthy. Act in a responsible way. Never do anything that would harm your relationship with the customers, either internally or externally.

Objectives and Managing Them

The starting point of any professional journey is to have a clear understanding of what you want to achieve in the short term and long term.

When you start to think about what you want to achieve, learn to differentiate between aims, aspirations, and objectives.

Aims or aspirations are typically subjective and intangible. They are not measurable.

Objectives are clearly measurable.

Once you have clarity on what you want to achieve, answer three vital questions:

1. How will you achieve it?
2. When will you achieve it?
3. How will you decide whether you have achieved it?

A simple technique to enrich your objective setting and execution can be to L.A.M.P them!!

L-Level of competency needed: Understand or estimate the level of competency you need to use to achieve your objective. Check for the gaps and have a plan to gain the required competency to achieve your objectives.

A-Actions needed: To achieve the defined objectives, you must initiate various actions; you will need to involve your customers, your team, or other stakeholders in these actions. The success of your objectives will depend on your preparedness to get engaged in these actions. You must also commit yourself to being part of the action initiated by other stakeholders.

M-Measurable: The objectives set must be clearly measurable. The units of measurement must be clearly defined and must not be ambiguous. For every defined objective, you should be able to decide if you achieved the objective on clear terms.

P-Possible Constraints: List the possible constraints that you may face, for achieving the defined objectives. These may be related to time, budget, or skills. Have a plan to overcome these constraints.

Be an eternal salesman

No matter what role you perform in your organization, you must learn to sell. What you sell need not necessarily be the products to external customers, but it can be your ideas, your contribution, or your point of view. This selling can be an internal activity, selling to your colleagues, bosses, and to other stakeholders. These are the people who can influence your growth in the organization.

Irrespective of your role and position in the organization, you must acquire basic selling skills.

Leaders with good selling skills grow faster in the organization.

Effective Conversation

Effective conversation is a must-have skill for young business professionals. It is a skill that helps you to efficiently control the conversation to optimize effectiveness during time constraints.

The purpose of effective conversation is to ensure that you receive and deliver quality information in a cordial environment. Your effective conversation skills will help others to open up to you with ease. For an effective conversation, you will need skills to ask the right type of questions along with good listening skills. You must practice the following to master effective conversation skills -

- Open questions
- Closed questions
- Reflector questions
- Test understanding questions
- Pause and silence
- Active listening
- Written notes
- Summaries

Open Question

The open question does not have a specific answer. The answers are openly told and are elaborate. The open questions always start with one of the following words –

- Who?
- What?
- Why?
- When?

- Where?
- Which?
- How?

Examples:

- Why did you approach us to get a quote?
- What do we need to do to make you feel comfortable?

Open questions should be used when you want your customers to respond openly. These questions will help develop a conversation easily, in the direction in which you want the conversation to go.

Closed questions

These questions have a specific answer, usually in a word or a sentence.

Example:

- Do we meet again on Saturday or Sunday?

Closed questions are asked when you ask the customer for the order in a direct way and you want an answer in "Yes," "No," or "I don't know."

Reflector Questions

A reflector question is a special type of short, open question, where the same words that have just been spoken in the last sentence are used.

Example:

Statement: "The product offered should have a shelf life that is very good."

<u>Reflector</u>: "Very good?"

With reflector questions, you are asking the other person to elaborate more on a specific point.

Reflector questions can be used at any time, normally used early in the call to convince your customer that you are keen and interested.

Avoid using numbers, names, and places as part of reflector questions. More than two reflector questions in a row may look insincere.

A good conversation will have more open and reflector questions and less closed questions.

Test understanding questions

These questions must be used to test your own understanding by making others clarify what they are trying to tell you.

Example:
"You said the panel should be painted blue on the front and red on the back?"

Or

"Have I understood it right that you want the panel to be painted in blue and red?"

Effective use of test understanding questions will greatly reduce verbal misunderstandings and apologies.

Pauses and silence:

Many times, in a conversation, when you are asking questions to others, they may want some time to think about the answer. Allow them to have the time to think and respond. Do not rush and interrupt their thinking. Remain silent as long as it takes. This is not an easy thing to do. But silence works.

Your question to the customer should be answered by the customer. Do not answer the question for him. Remain silent till he answers, as long as it may take.

Remaining silent at the right time during a conversation is a technique and it requires practice.

Active Listening:

It is very important to be perceived as an active listener by other people whom you are in conversation with. The right use of questions and silence, along with positive body language will do the job.

Written Notes:
These should be short and only to the point. Taking down notes should not distract the conversation.

Summary:
A summary goes over the conversation you have already covered in brief points which are important for both the parties involved. A good summary is often a platform for the conversation to advance positively.

Summaries are helpful during conversations to –

- Establish understanding for both the people in conversation of what has been covered till now and what needs to be covered.
- Control the conversation.
- Give you time for thinking and planning for your next move, especially during difficult conversations.

Negotiation skills

Negotiation means that two parties are in the process of reaching some sort of agreement or solution in a fixed time frame.

We all negotiate on a daily basis. We negotiate with our family members, and with vendors when we buy stuff in markets, in office work, and in many other places. Some people are naturally good at it and some people will need to practice it. Business negotiations must be more structured and focused. The stakes are higher with wider implications.

Business negotiations start much before parties start to discuss the solution or a settlement. Business negotiations have the following phases –

- Prepare
- Discuss
- Propose
- Bargain
- Close deal

Businesses today need to be constantly prepared to negotiate. They will need to be clear on what they need to gain and what they are willing to let go of. They need to build on the leverages and relationships which can be used during the bargain and close deal phases.

During the first three phases, do all the research you can on the market situation, competition, and the party that you will enter the negotiation with. Understand how the other party perceives, defines, and measures "value." Always start with a realistic, negotiable offer. All areas of potential conflicts need to be understood and clarified during this phase.

Once the position of each party is clear on the things that are being negotiated, and there is clarity on the part that needs agreement, the bargaining phase starts. No new areas of conflict should emerge once the bargaining starts.

During the bargaining phase, always try to reach a "win–win" situation. Conduct your negotiations in such a way that they focus on business values and issues and avoid imposing your viewpoint and opinion on the other party. In business negotiations, there is no scope for personal or emotional attacks.

Ensure that there is a two-way movement in the bargaining process. Make concessions only when you must, do not make them for the sake of it. Never give anything away, always trade concessions for something in return. Ensure that you have locked out your competitors or at least know their progress. It is likely that you will face an entirely different set of people during the bargaining phase and during the closing sale phase. Engage with the right level of people based on who from the other party is engaged. Promises for tomorrow are very pleasant to hear and easy getaways. Do not accept any promises in words. Ask for a written commitment to see if the other party is serious.

Understand the negotiation dynamics of the other party. Read the negotiating styles of the negotiators and the roles they play in the negotiation. Use appropriate skill and style during the close deal phase.

During the close deal phase, look out for some form of commitment or buying signals from the other party. At the close deal stage, you must negotiate only with the person who has the authority to make a decision. From your side, you must be fully prepared with the simulation of various scenarios or business cases so that you can make a decision if the other party has a proposal that can be considered.

Some techniques commonly used by negotiators are –

The Traders Close:

Use this early, during the close deal phase negotiation, to test the waters. This is done knowing very well that it may be unrealistic to get an agreement at this stage, but you would never know till you ask.

Example:
Customer: Does your company provide a warranty for 48 months?

Traders Close: Suppose, if my company were able to provide 48 months of warranty, would I be prepared to close the deal now?

The alternate close:
Here, the customer is presented with alternatives by you. The customer is given a feeling that he is in charge. Though this can be used at any time during the call, it is more than often used at the final stage of the sale. This helps to draw the customer into the final and positive "go-ahead" decision.

Example:
Would you like to see our models on Tuesday or Wednesday?
Which one would you prefer, red or blue?

Direct close:
This is a straightforward way of closing a deal. Just ask your customer if you have an agreement. This is only possible when the parties have had an elaborate bargain phase, with two-way movement, and both parties making concessions on their positions.

Example:
"Sir, as discussed in the last meeting, we can accept a 48-month warranty if you agree to increase the advance payment to 30%. Do I have your approval to go ahead and process the order?"

Roles people play:
During the negotiation process, as part of the preparation, you must figure out the roles of the negotiators from other parties involved in the negotiation. There are 4 key roles that the negotiators have.
King: The decision maker, who has money, authority, and need. The final negotiation should only be done with the king. Your success will often depend on how fast you identify the king in the negotiation map and contact him. Many times, the king is not visible or involved in the early phases of negotiations. He is likely to surface during the close deal phase.

Prime Minister:

He is somebody on whom the king relies on to take the decision and values his input. The prime minister can be outside the organization. Many times, prime ministers are not visibly active during the early phases of negotiations. They may be present during the meetings but not noticeable.

Witch:

He is someone close to the king and can often create doubts in the mind of the King by highlighting some disadvantages in your offer or referring to one-off failures for bad references. He does this to score with the king and not necessarily with any other purpose in mind. He is somebody who is eyeing the position of prime minister and wants to demonstrate his influence on the king. It is also possible that he is not in favor of your company for reasons that are best known to him.

Soldier:

He is the first person that you meet during the proposal and preparation phases. He decides if he wants to allow you to meet the king. You must pass through this person before you can meet the king. More often than not you cannot avoid them on your road to reach the king. He is powerful and he can decide who gets to meet the king and when.

Negotiation Styles

Style 1: Mitr: (Friend/Buddy)

The people with this negotiation style are very friendly and courteous. They always make you feel comfortable. You need to be aware that they are friendly to all, even your competitors. You will easily misjudge the effectiveness of the meeting with them. When you finish the negotiation meetings with people who have this style of negotiation, you will always walk out with a good feeling, even when difficult topics are discussed. If you do not recognize the negotiation style, you end up giving more to them than getting from them. They are very smart negotiators.

The most effective way to negotiate with Mitr (Buddy) style is to adopt the same style and be firm on your position till you get what you need in return. Be friendly and courteous all the while. Avoid any kind of aggression in actions or words. Avoid speaking ill about your competitors, focus only on your strengths.

Style 2: Nana-ji: (Grand Father/Old school

The people with this style of negotiation consider everything new, everything latest, with suspension. They are old school and "old is gold" for them. They will only consider proven things with heritage and tradition. New technology is generally off-limits.

The most effective way to deal with such a style is to highlight the heritage, experience, and number of years that you and your company have been in business for. Avoid pitching any new technology. Avoid using words like latest/state-of-the-art technology/first time in the industry. Rather, start your conversation with how experienced your company is and how the technology you are using has evolved over a period of time. Try to pitch this as an evolution rather than an invention.

Style 3: Dewan-ji (Accountant/ Check-all)

For people with this style of negotiation, you will need to provide proof of all the claims you make. They do not believe in claims or statements. Marketing gimmicks and sales talks do not work with them.

The most effective way to negotiate with Dewan-ji (Check-all) style is to have the necessary proof of all the product advantages you claim. Provide sufficient endorsements, variable references, test certificates, and quality inspection certificates. Insist that they verify all the proof and documents provided. This will enhance their confidence in your proposal.

Style 4: Dalapati: (Commander / Pushy)

People with this style of negotiation like to dominate. They have a mindset of "my way or highway." They believe it is the "seat of power" and would like to deal with you from a higher ego position. They generally have a short span of attention. They do not get into details by themselves. They are impatient for results and quick decision-makers. They are trustworthy. They do not like negative answers. They do have the urge to always win and maintain the image of a winner.

The most effective way to negotiate with a commander is first to match their energy levels and then to pace their tone of speech. Be firm and direct with your reply. Maintain eye contact. Be polite but firm. Stand your ground with a smile and do not blink. Make an argument about how he would be a winner if he chooses your proposal. Make sure that the final say is from him and make him feel like a winner. Normally, you would not get a second chance. Close the deal on the first attempt. Choose your words, have short and effective conversations, and remember that you have a short span of his attention. If they do not like you in the first three minutes of your conversation, you have very little chance to impress them during the latter part of the meeting.

Managing Objections:

Managing objections is a skill that is helpful in all stages of negotiations and conversations. Objections are business opportunities. They need to be handled well.

During negotiations, when you are not able to reach any agreement, you must check on what are the objections from your customers which are stopping your customer from reaching the agreement. List down all the objections and categorize them under the following labels –

- Doubts
- Misunderstandings
- Genuine disadvantages

There is a definite way of handling each one of these. Always try to understand the true meaning of the objection of the customer, by asking more questions.

Listen to all the objections from the customer and then try to make a commitment from the customer that if you agree on the management of the objection, "Can we go ahead?" Be calm, slow down, be thorough, and show that you respect and care. Stick to the structure.

Doubt:

If the objection is a doubt, give the proof and proceed towards closing the call. When a customer seems and sounds doubtful, unsure, frowns, and looks puzzled, ask him what he is unsure of and find the best way to clear his doubt. Then provide the required proof.

Misunderstanding:

If the objection is because of a misunderstanding, apologize, clarify, and proceed toward closing the call.

Misunderstanding occurs when the communication is not good enough. If the misunderstanding is because of miscommunication, identify the error and put it right, and move ahead. Don't invite objections due to poor communication or silly mistakes.

Genuine disadvantages:

If the objection is because of a genuine disadvantage of your product, there is very little you can do at the negotiation stage. In such a situation, you must try to maximize the benefits of your product and minimize the disadvantages that are being highlighted as an objection.

This is the most difficult of the objections to manage. First, test the understanding of the customer. Make sure the customer is making a fair and correct comparison with your competitors. Once you are clear on the objection and its merit, put forth a defense, highlighting the over superiority of your product, and it can score over the disadvantage which you must acknowledge as minor.

Use of AI

Artificial intelligence is "the next internet." It will dramatically change the way you work. It is a disruptive technological tool that is here to stay.

Get used to this new technology. Learn to use this technology for your benefit. Depending on your skill sets and your role in your organization, learning AI must not be treated as an option but a necessity to avoid redundancy affecting you. AI will make many of the current job profiles redundant.

Evaluate how AI is affecting your job now and how it may affect it in the future. Understanding AI and its likely impact will help you get prepared for the next big thing and be a step ahead of redundancy.

AI is an opportunity if you get to know of it today. It will become a threat to you tomorrow if you fail to sync yourself with this new technology.

My Notes:

What are 3 skills that I will need to improve/acquire to power my career to the next level?

1.
2.
3.

How will I acquire these skills?

1.
2.
3.

Chapter 5: Prepare for the Greater Good

The Greater Good

There are many good things that happen due to the profitable existence of a business entity in society. It provides employment to the people around and is a means of livelihood for them. The profitable company pays taxes, and its expansion helps the local economy further.

As an employee of a company, it is your duty to ensure that you do all that you can, legally, to ensure that your company does continue to exist profitably. The company must exist for society and not the other way around.

Being an employee of the company does not mean that you become blind to all your responsibilities towards society and the environment. Being an employee of a company does not mean that you are obliged to stay silent on the topics that should be spoken of. If you do not speak up on the topics which should be spoken of, you are not helping your company but harming it. Your responsibility as an employee is also to ensure that your company keeps up all the promises to the community and society and does follow all the good practices within the legal framework to ensure the greater good for the community and humanity.

Keep your character intact, always.

Ignite a Purpose

The workplace is a great example of a diverse group of people with different backgrounds, different religions, different languages, and different cultures coming together for the common purpose of profitability and striving to achieve the same.

It may be true that the main, common drive for most people will be financial stability and growth, which of course is very correct and necessary.

As a leader, you can take this beyond if you manage to ignite the purpose of the greater good among the people you are working with. This ignition can be to do more, do better, for society. Ignite a purpose to change for the better. Ignite a purpose to contribute to society.

Look for opportunities to influence change in the people and community for the better. These efforts will be seen as social leadership and will help your company get recognized as a brand that supports the community. This can be a key influencer when socially aware people make purchases and recommendations.

Training and Internal Internships

Never lose an opportunity to get an upgrade on your skills or accelerated experiences, either laterally or vertically. If opportunities are difficult to come by, you must find a way to get to them.

Be in close contact with your HR business partner. Ask for opportunities from your HR or line manager. At the beginning of your career, it may be a good idea even to bargain for a training or accelerated experience internship instead of a salary hike. This has multiple advantages. You will look like a guy who values growth over monetary benefits. Accelerated experience can do wonders for your career.

Try to get as much training as possible early in your career. This is when you are eager to learn and absorb without prejudice.

Listen to What is Not Said

Early in your career, you are likely to be told "what to do" and "how to do it" by your supervisor or manager. Do not get into the habit of waiting for instructions to perform a task.

You must learn to anticipate and be ready to perform or complete the task before being told. You must develop awareness and be alert about what is happening around you. The trick here is to learn to listen beyond what is told.

Generally, managers have little patience and may only have enough time to assign a task to you. They can also be vague while detailing a few things. You must learn to understand what is being stated subtly, what are the words that were used by a specific manager, and what they mean in the context. Clarify your understanding just to make sure.

Professional Networking

Put your effort and develop a professional network within and outside your organization. Reach out to people at all levels. The professional social media platform is a good way to start. Interact with key contacts on a personal basis, and professionally.

Reach out to these contacts -

- for advice
- for suggestions
- for participating in discussions
- for sharing your learnings
- for asking professional questions

Avoid -

- forwards and spamming
- avoid subjects related to politics religion, and other personal beliefs
- sharing personal pictures or commenting on personal pictures

Your network is your net worth – Porter Gale

Emotional Intelligence

The term "emotional intelligence" was coined in 1990 by researchers John Mayer and Peter Salovey. It may take some effort to fully understand what that term means.

Emotional intelligence can be defined as the capacity to be aware of, control, and express one's emotions, and to handle interpersonal relationships judiciously and empathetically.

Emotions are key initiators of actions and reactions. They make you move. You act when you feel an emotion and want to do something about it. Emotions of all kinds are always generated in our interaction with this world as we know it.

One who is aware of these emotions and manages or masters to understand, regulate and use the emotions, will be looked upon as a leader.

The core competencies of a person that influence his emotional intelligence are -

- Motivation
- Empathy for others
- Ability to regulate emotions
- Awareness of one's emotions
- Social skills to manage emotions of self and others

In order to improve your emotional intelligence levels, you will need to work on the above core competencies.

You can begin with the following -

Emotional Awareness: Apart from being aware of your strengths and weaknesses. You will need to be aware of what effect your emotions have on your and the team's performance.

Manage emotions: This is about how you manage your emotions in stressful and difficult situations and during setbacks.

Social Behavior: Along with understanding your own emotions, you will need to have empathy for others' emotions. You will need to learn to read the emotions around you and respond accordingly.

Relationship Management: You will need to learn how to manage emotions and have the ability to influence your own and others' emotions in a variety of situations and to resolve conflicts.

Start work on improving emotional intelligence. It helps.

- Emotional intelligence is a key leadership trait that is needed for success in mid and senior-level positions.
- When you start your career, normally you earn your first couple of promotions based on your technical skills, however for you to reach a mid and senior level in the organization, you will need to demonstrate your emotional intelligence trait.
- Emotional intelligence is what sets high performers apart from peers with similar technical skills and knowledge.
- Over the years, emotional intelligence has become a key performance indicator for leadership positions.

"Emotional intelligence is the key to both personal and professional success."

Work-Life Balance

Different people need different levels of work-life balance. This will also depend on different stages of your career and life progress.

There is no "one dress fits all" type of work-life balance structure. You will need to find your own balance, based on what you value in your life and how you want your life to get shaped.

For people in their early careers, I would recommend that you focus and take time out for the below.

Self:

- Work on the fitness of the body and mind.
- Work on your hobby.
- Have fun, and party with friends responsibly.
- Work on personality development and life skills.

Family and friends

- Network with family and friends.
- Celebrate and share happiness and success.
- Be there when family and friends need you.
- Develop a strong emotional bond with people you care for and with people that care for you.

Society:

- Give back to society in any way you can.
- Giving money is not enough, try to engage physically and emotionally. You can start by helping in an orphanage or old age home or volunteer in hospitals.
- Mentor underprivileged kids and guide them to find success.

A career is not life, it is a means to live your life, on your own terms.

How to Use "Feedback."

You will receive feedback from people around you and more, all the time. Below are some tips on how to manage the feedback -

- Encourage people to give feedback. You must seek voluntary feedback from some key people that matter. Your mentor, manager, teammates, subordinates, and other colleagues that you would interact with.
- Learn to distinguish between "opinions," "criticism," and "feedback." Feedback is balanced and actionable.
- Accept all the feedback with humility and do not react when the feedback is being given. If you are not clear on some points, do seek clarification for a better understanding of what the person wants to convey. Do not justify your actions at this stage.
- Irrespective of whether the feedback is positive or negative, ask the person how he thinks "you could have done it better/how to improve."
- List all the actionable feedback and prioritize the ones you want to act upon. Do not feel compelled to change just because you received certain feedback.

Feedback is those invisible hands that will shape the mold of your career. Be flexible to change but firm enough to keep the shape.

My Notes:

What are the 3 things I can do to prepare myself to show leadership to contribute to the greater good?

1.
2.
3.

Chapter 6: Habits to Kill

Procrastination

Procrastination, in simple terms, is the habit of postponing some tasks till the last moment or beyond deadlines, knowing very well the negative consequences of such an irrational delay in starting/completing the task. Instead of engaging with the tasks at hand, you prioritize some trivial tasks or the ones you like to do over what you should be doing.

Everybody procrastinates on some tasks sometimes, which should be okay and manageable. However, if this becomes a chronic habit, you are sure to experience a negative impact.

Chronic procrastination can pull you back on your career or will restrict the growth potential that you otherwise could have reached.

Procrastination starts when you start choosing the tasks that give you instant gratification over the tasks that would give you benefits in the long term. The other way to put it is you decide to do the tasks you enjoy doing rather than doing the tasks that need to be completed and will have a negative impact if not completed.

If you have begun to procrastinate, pull yourself out of this. It is not easy though. Some tips on how to come out of the procrastination habit are –

- Think of the long-term benefits of completing the task.
- Think of tasks as something that needs to be completed rather than something that you need to enjoy.
- Be ruthless with yourself as a project manager. (I have emphasized several times in this book that project management skill is one of the must-have skills in the corporate world.)

Reward yourself with some trivial tasks after you complete a key milestone on your must-do task. This way you will not miss the part of instant gratification.

Hate losing.

Have a sense of competition and know that your competitor right now will be working on the tasks and is likely to beat you only because you choose not to work on the task and not because he is more capable.

Work with a mentor or in a group where you make a habit of announcing the progress on the task and the reason for the delay with full honesty.

Do not play for the audience

Corporate work is not a platform for entertainment, even though you may find an audience for your act. The biggest quality of the audience is that they are only emotionally connected to the stage and not rationally. The taste and preference change, and you have no control over that. The audience will make you believe what they want you to believe. They clap and you feel you are doing good and if they boo you feel that you are not doing what they expected from you.

In the corporate world, you are not expected to entertain and hence need to be rational and logical and not succumb to admirers or haters. Do not change your script to please your audience. You need to show what needs to be shown, no matter how it looks. Remember, you are here to be effective and not to gain short-term popularity.

Do not fall for the pseudo-audience.

Off-the-cuff remarks

Off-the-cuff remarks are made without much thought. They are spontaneous and, most of the time, are not intentional. "Off-the-cuff" remarks can be fun when they are made with a group of friends, but they are not fun when you make it with your colleagues.

In a business environment, you are supposed to say only what you mean. Off-the-cuff remarks can get you into trouble sooner or later. Your colleagues will start judging you for what you say. There is a good chance that they will misinterpret your remark and gossip about you later. Your colleagues will not express themselves when you are around as they would fear getting an off-the-cuff remark from you. You do not want them to start avoiding you.

Prejudice

Carrying any prejudice in the business world can never be good for your career. Having a preconceived evaluation or classification of a person, based on their personal characteristics, will pull you away from making rational decisions. It is one quality a leader in the business world cannot have.

Many may even be unaware of the prejudices they have. Prejudice is a natural and normal process for humans and hence is a hidden factor in the personal decision-making process of a person. The natural decision-making process, with all the built-in prejudice, may have even worked well for a person in conservative and non-cosmopolitan environments.

In a business environment, which is global in nature, you will interact with people from multiple genders, nationalities, colors, religions, political affiliations, etc. You must keep a "filter" for prejudice and make sure they are kept away from your business decision-making. Activate your filter when you react or feel in a particular way about a person.

Be aware that you can be prejudiced in both positive and negative ways. In simple terms, you need to check if you are feeling favorable or unfavorable towards a person or a thing without prior experience, or rational and reliable inputs to do so.

Comfort Zone

As a young executive, you must keep getting out of your comfort zone to have a meaningful career.

A comfort zone gives you an illusion of stability and happiness. How do you know if you are trapped in a comfort zone? Look out for the signs. In your comfort zone –

- You are not learning anything new.
- You are not being challenged.
- You are getting used to a routine.
- You are trapped with the tag of an expert to make yourself averse to changes and challenges.
- You are in a danger zone in your career.

In today's digital world, technology is a positive disruption. It's always a risk that our current skills, best practices, and knowledge may become obsolete faster than we can imagine. When such disruptions happen, people in their comfort zone will find it difficult to navigate their careers in the competitive business world.

Your comfort zone will fool you by giving you a false sense of worthiness and will prevent you from taking any action which will move you away from your comfort zone. You will start fearing the risk of failure and humiliation as you have little or no experience of failure in your comfort zone. It is better to fail sooner rather than later. Your ability to handle failure and imbibe learning adds to your character growth, which you will miss in your comfort zone.

My Notes:

What are the 3 habits of mine that I want to kill?

1.
2.
3.

Chapter 7: Diamond in the Market

Value yourself

As a young executive, you are constantly adding skills and learning new techniques. Naturally, you are adding value to yourself. If you can use these skills and learnings to contribute to the better performance of your company, then you are becoming an asset to your company. This also means that you are now more valuable in the market as a talent.

You are a "Diamond in the Market!"

Make it an annual exercise to update your CV. Check your value in the market, even if you do not intend to change your job now.

Never allow anyone to take advantage of you or make you do things that you do not agree with. Your freedom and your pride are your most valuable assets which you should defend at any cost.

Negotiate

Never hesitate to negotiate with your peers and the leadership for the resources that you need to perform. You must negotiate to get the resources you need. Do not be under the impression that the leadership will not be happy if you start a negotiation. If you are negotiating for the resources, it will be looked at in a positive way. If you negotiate for the things that are needed, it will give the impression that you are managing the task professionally.

Do not hesitate to negotiate benefits or a salary hike during your annual appraisal. Like for any negotiation, be well prepared to highlight your impact on the business and your development as a leader. Highlight the learnings you have had and ask for higher responsibilities. Provide an action plan of the feedback you get for the improvement.

Negotiate for what you feel is rightfully yours. Do it professionally. Remember, it's always the crying baby that gets fed first.

Be Visible

Being humble doesn't mean being invisible. Visibility is key for growth in corporate structure. When you do good work that produces good results, be sure to take credit for it. If your idea has contributed to the business's success, do talk about it, and take due credit.

If you are part of a team that has achieved success, talk about the contribution of each of your team members and give due credit for their contribution. Remember, nobody wants to be invisible. Do not forget to talk about yourself and your learnings.

Visibility and spotlight bring responsibility and challenges. It will make sure that you organize yourself so that you can be seen doing your best to achieve results. It also brings pressure and stress if you do not manage the challenges well.

Visibility for you is the same as spotting a potential star performer for the leadership team.

Diamonds need to shine!

When to change your job:
As a young executive, you must remember that the normal career span of an individual is, on average, 30 years! It's a long journey! It needs to be enjoyed. Changing jobs is one of the key events that will influence this journey and also how it ends.

You need to plan your career and execute it properly. The last 10 years of your career is the phase of your exponential growth. To reach this launch pad for exponential growth, you must be careful with your decisions on job changes in the first 20 years.

There are fewer positions at the top. The challenges, rewards, and recognitions are multiple times compared to what is available for lower and mid-levels. It takes time to reach the top and not everyone can reach the top. It needs planning and luck.

You should start thinking about changing your job –

- If your current job is getting routine and you are no longer being challenged.
- If you are not learning anything new.
- If you are not growing in your current company either with higher responsibilities or critical projects.
- If your company values have changed and are not aligned with your personal values anymore.
- If you see that the company is not performing financially well consistently for 3 years.

When you are approached by another organization for a job. This is a good situation for you. This means that your skills are in demand in your market and the market values your skills. However, if you are approached to do the same work that you were doing in your current job, you should think twice before accepting it. Some questions that you should answer before you accept the new job is –

- Is this in line with my mid- and long-term career planning?
- What value addition and job enrichment will happen with the new job?
- What will I miss if I leave my current job?
- Why am I needed in the new company?
- What kind of leadership will I be interacting with?
- Are the values of the company aligned with my personal values?
- How will I grow in the next 3 years in the new company?

The comfort zone is where careers are buried.

My Notes:

What are the 3 things that will make me a diamond in the market?

1.
2.
3.

About the Author

Vivek Puranik is an engineering graduate with a master's degree in management systems from a reputed Indian university. He is passionate about grooming young talent. He has rich and practical experience of over 27 years with global elevator corporations across the globe, spanning India, UAE, Bahrain, Italy, and the USA. He is currently located in the USA with his wife and two kids. He is also a published poet in the Kannada language.

www.ingramcontent.com/pod-product-compliance
Lightning Source LLC
LaVergne TN
LVHW041112150826
845673LV00007B/2022

* 9 7 9 8 8 9 0 2 6 7 4 4 3 *